Dreaming Wonders

Edited By Lynsey Evans

First published in Great Britain in 2024 by:

Young Writers
Remus House
Coltsfoot Drive
Peterborough
PE2 9BF
Telephone: 01733 890066
Website: www.youngwriters.co.uk

FOREWORD

Welcome Reader, to a world of dreams.

For Young Writers' latest competition, we asked our writers to dig deep into their imagination and create a poem that paints a picture of what they dream of, whether it's a make-believe world full of wonder or their aspirations for the future.

The result is this collection of fantastic poetic verse that covers a whole host of different topics. Let your mind fly away with the fairies to explore the sweet joy of candy lands, join in with a game of fantasy football, or you may even catch a glimpse of a unicorn or another mythical creature. Beware though, because even dreamland has dark corners, so you may turn a page and walk into a nightmare!

Whereas the majority of our writers chose to stick to a free verse style, others gave themselves the challenge of other techniques such as acrostics and rhyming couplets.

Each piece in this collection shows the writers' dedication and imagination – we truly believe that seeing their work in print gives them a well-deserved boost of pride, and inspires them to keep writing, so we hope to see more of their work in the future!

CONTENTS

East Hunsbury Primary School, Northampton

Dorothy Yates (10)	61
Sophie Lah-Anyane (9)	62
Lexie Sloanes-Ford (8)	63
Jessica Santhosh (11)	64
Matteo Angella (9)	66
Ethan Elliott (8)	67
Milan Protasiewicz (9)	68
Olivia Green (10)	69
Lucy Lucan (9)	70
Emily Macey (8)	71
Sofia Pilipciuk (9)	72
Gloria M (9)	73
Meryem Akaslan (9)	74
Freya Hoskins (10)	75
Lucy Catling (9)	76
Tate McMahon (10)	78
Hannah Macey (10)	79
Maya Dobranici (9)	80
Oliver Barbour (9)	81
Reyes Paynton-White (11)	82
Lottie Chapman (9)	83
Clara Taylor (10)	84
Millie Leighton	85
Yash Singh (11)	86
Poppy Cook (9)	87
Millie Kremenskas (7)	88
Laura M (11)	89
Thomas Barley (9)	90
Eadie Keeley	91
Amelia Aran (10)	92
Zachary Boodhoo (9)	93
Blake Coote (9)	94
Hayyan Sardar (10)	95
Harrison Balneaves (10)	96
Joshua Whitnall (9)	97
Aliyah-Mae Kelly (10)	98
Morgan Cosford (10)	99
Carolyn Juan Anil (9)	100
Jessica Irons (11)	101
Victor Puscausu (11)	102
Madalina Turculet (10)	103
Jansen Thompson (8)	104
Tatum Bradshaw (10)	105
Ollie Bradshaw (10)	106
Shea Chambers (10)	107
Alfie Clark (9)	108
Milly Webb (10)	109
Erika Maria Ursu (9)	110
Chloe Sayers (10)	111
James Kimber (10)	112
Scarlett Stockman (9)	113
Lillian Ibeh (11)	114
Milly Benson (11)	115
Daisy Gericke (8)	116
Mikey Ayub	117
Ava Wild (8)	118
Jason Wright (10)	119
Lexi Greenwood-Walden (11)	120
Inna Monita (10)	121
Matilda Barr (11)	122
Henry Elliot (10)	123
Mia Kremenskaite (10)	124
Daniel Dawodu (10)	125
Isla Husbands (8)	126
Castalella Zarzuela-Newey (10)	127
George Mantelis (10)	128
Sophie Trigg (7)	129
Ezekiel Gill (8)	130
Oliver Clements-Hill (11)	131
Louix Faulkner (9)	132
Sophie Elkington (8)	133
Millie Parsonson (7)	134
Sophie Godwin (10)	135
David Pasere (7)	136
Ella Stonhill (10)	137
Charlotte Irons (8)	138
Noah Pickering (11)	139
Victoria Cegolea (10)	140
Charlie Maddison (10)	141
Mason Kremenskas (9)	142
Charlie Ratcliffe (11)	143
Thomas Barbour (10)	144
Olivia Kelly (8)	145
Ryley Jwanczuk (10)	146

| Emily Griffiths (9) | 147 |
| Luisa Matayoshi Marchesin (7) | 148 |

Gladestry Church-In-Wales Primary School, Kington

Skye James (9)	149
Nia Price (10)	150
Meredith Robinson	151
Albie Jones (10)	152
Wyn Daman Thomas (8)	153
Cian Tolley (10)	154
Tom James (10)	155
Rowan Vincent (9)	156
Daniel Lloyd (11)	157
Lyra Parry (9)	158
Sofia Hodge (10)	159
Lili Davies (10)	160
Eli Knight (8)	161
Florence Jauncey-Wellard (8)	162
Wilbur Fraser (7)	163
Huw Stafford Tolley (10)	164
Callum Price (8)	165
Ben James (7)	166
Teddy James (8)	167

Plymtree CE Primary School, Plymtree

Lacey Louise (10)	168
Alastair North (7)	169
Daisy Spicer (7)	170
Dexter Spicer (8)	171
Emily Blade (9)	172

Regent House Prepartory School, Newtownards

Sophie White (10)	173
Nina Miller (10)	174
Rose Harper (11)	176
Hannah Poulter (11)	178
Tom Holroyd (11)	179
Darcy Gray (9)	180

Marla Gilmore (9)	181
Alexander Clements (9)	182
Jude O'Hara (11)	183
Emilie Park (8)	184
Ruby-Rose Roberts (10)	185
Christine Large (10)	186
Ella McDowell (9)	187
Katie Turner (9)	188
Bruce Rothwell (10)	189
William Rankin (9)	190
Cillian Steensma (8)	191

THE POEMS

The World Of Unicorns

One day in school,
I looked magical and cool,
The holiday came,
And it was rain,
In my sister's school,
They had shown them the world of glitter unicorns,
I felt excited to explore it all,
My eyes were light.

My sister said, "Let's go and find the unicorn world,"
I said, "If there will be any unicorns, because I love green,"
"There will be unicorns and I promise I'll show you them,"
I know it wasn't real,
But there wasn't anything interesting for a holiday.

So, we went to find it,
You won't believe that we found it,
Every single thing was magical,
That was fantastical,
And after that, I know nothing's impossible,
You just have to believe in yourself.

Sakshi Dhanai (10)
Aldborough Primary School, Ilford

A Nightmare

The dream always turns into a nightmare,
No matter what I do,
I just want to keep living in my dream,
Instead of waking up to a nightmare,
So much is going on in my closet,
Every time I open it,
Blackening, whirling, scary ghosts and darkness,
The nightmare has returned!

It's haunting me,
Shivers crawling up my spine,
Heart racing and pounding,
And there's nowhere to hide,
I did it, I made it back to bed,
Time to go back to sleep,
I'm finally back to being me.

Suddenly, I wake up sweating,
And screaming,
It's already early morning,
And I was dreaming...

Aaliyah Ahmed (10)
Aldborough Primary School, Ilford

My Dream To Space

My dream is to go to space,
Where I could build a secret base,
In space, I'll jump as high as I can,
Higher, higher as high as a van,
There's plenty of space to do whatever I wish,
100% I'm going to go mental-ish,
Imagine hearing no sound,
Imagine a place where no human can be found,
There's going to be so many planets to see,
When I come back I'm going to be full of glee,
Imagine seeing Mercury, that'll be amazing,
But I badly want to see Neptune, beautiful glazing,
I'm all ready, well not fully ready,
Who is going to take care of the aliens?

Salaar Khan (10)
Aldborough Primary School, Ilford

Nightmare

N othing worse than a horrible dream,

I n the middle of nowhere, I took a breath,

G etting lost in terrors of dark, I remembered the ghost stories from the park,

H oping they may disappear,

T haaa! A noise of horror I went to check,

M y goodness, a blood-covered creature,

A rghh! It's trying to choke me!

R attling commotion came from the ground,

E erie eyes drop, so I decided to close mine,

S udden silence began, my eyes opened in relief, I was still in bed.

Zainab Ali Zaidi (10)
Aldborough Primary School, Ilford

My Magical Dreams

The day goes by and the night comes,
I run and jump, it's time for fun,
Tuck and rock, it's time to sleep,
My magical dreams fly in from the deep,
Today, a firefighter,
Tomorrow my own hero,
The never-ending fun,
It feels like I've won,
I don't want it to end,
I want to go on,
Forever and ever,
In my dreams,
The fruits taste so sweet,
I feel I could take on an entire fleet,
It's time to wake,
But it's not the end,
Just a start to many more adventures.

Tioluwani Oladele (11)
Aldborough Primary School, Ilford

Chinese Wonders

C alm, soft clouds,
H igh up in the sky,
I ce lollies drifting around me,
N ice Chinese food with ramen,
E asy dragon-making for the Lunar New Year,
S inister cats next to me,
E arly tea and super plans.

D rastic fire dancing around me,
R ude ninjas, saying mean things,
A nd who could forget about the calm,
G ong strikes on the Lunar New Year,
O yster slurps in the city,
N ow goodbye, be calm and relax.

Eduard Diaconu (8)
Aldborough Primary School, Ilford

Arsenal FC

D own in Arsenal FC, the Arsenal manager signed me and Ednilson, we were happy, this was our dream

'R ound about 5:30pm, Ed and I made our debut and the stadium was as shiny as ever

E dnilson scored five goals, I scored six goals

A fter the match, our team, Arsenal FC, won the Champions League

M y dreams were accomplished

I n the dressing room, everyone was celebrating and no one went to bed

N umber seven I got

G ame week number seven.

Brandon Niyi-Otiko (8)
Aldborough Primary School, Ilford

Fairy Tale

F ind life in a fairy-tale dream.

A nd a fairy tale that you think isn't real, more than real,

I n the fairy tale is a total glow-up.

R are fairies fly around me as I'm special.

Y ou may have already seen the beautiful land.

T hat is my favourite part of this fairy tale.

A ll I can think of is my magical dream.

L ike I dreamed.

E njoy the beautiful weather, everyone is friendly.

Dream is a theme!

Elisa Katine (9)
Aldborough Primary School, Ilford

The Tree To Mystery

As I was staring at a bewitching basement,
I fell asleep in amazement.
After a tranquil nap from 3 o'clock,
My dream was terminated by a knock.

My inquisitiveness got the best of me,
I opened the door and saw an enormous tree,
It was growing instantaneous that I couldn't see.
There was a queue to reach the top,
If I wanted to climb it I would,
Try to be vigilant to not drop.

I got the courage, I climbed this tree,
This will be a journey.

Haziq Rizwan (10)
Aldborough Primary School, Ilford

Pirates Or Marines?

Into a world of my own,
Everyone arrived one by one.
Getting lost, a fear I see,
Never in the life of a pirate at sea.

The compass had broken,
And the clock had frozen.
What ship was I on?
Was it the Marines'?

I rushed through the doors,
While I heard loud roars.
I saw it, the flag,
But I was in rags.

It was the Marines',
But surely I wasn't to be seen.
I woke up,
And realised it was all a bad dream.

Maryam Khonat (11)
Aldborough Primary School, Ilford

Badminton

B am! I hit the shuttlecock with a slam!

A nd my enemy hits back, wham!

"D on't give up now you're so close,"

"M aybe I relax," but then he's frozen,

"I 'm a winner!" I boast,

N either he nor the crowd applaud me,

T he referee has a broad smile,

"O f course! I've really won!"

N ever did I realise that the match was never done!

Hana Butt (11)
Aldborough Primary School, Ilford

Unanswerable Zeus

The sky is sparkly and sapphire-blue,
It really depends on his mood,
Zeus, mighty Zeus, the god who rules,
Has been called a terribly vicious fool!

When Zeus is devastated,
Nothing is right!
The sky is too tall if clouds wander off,
And the worst is when you'll only see night!

Thunder and lightning crashes on our warm land,
When the weather is uncontrollable,
Zeus is mad!

Birha Khan (11)
Aldborough Primary School, Ilford

The Cheerleader Life

I can see pom-poms waving around,
I am in a basketball stadium,
I am with my friend Iman,
I feel pleasurable for this honour,
We all perform and do our best moves,
Iman and I are the leaders of the group,
We always have celebration parties with movies,
The crowd cheers for joy,
We all say oh boy,
Even the door cheers with joy when someone walks
into the room,
The crowd is screaming.

Ireoluwatomiwa Oladele (9)
Aldborough Primary School, Ilford

A Dream Of Dreams

Dreams can be dreamy,
All vibrant and shiny,
Filled with royalty.

Dreams can be scary,
With screams that can be eerie,
They are called nightmares, really,
With monsters that look shaggy.

Dreams can be emotional,
The opposite of fundamental,
But some of those dreams have a moral.

The moral is that dreams might come true,
So come and join the dreaming crew!

Baiza Jabeen (10)
Aldborough Primary School, Ilford

Football Man United

F un is football scoring.

O ranges are good for you and for footballers.

O wning lots of money which footballers own.

T rying to win football games which Man United do best.

B all is going around everywhere.

A pples are good for footballers.

L etting teammates score goals.

L ifting weights in the club gym. Being famous and having lots of money.

Arjun Dail (9)

Aldborough Primary School, Ilford

Dragon

D ragons are magical and fascinating,
R oaring louder than a lion, they will have you for their feasts,
A nd they are quite scary but loving,
G reat, they are, but humans are what they love to eat,
O n Dragon Land, new babies are born every day,
N othing can outsmart these dangerous, strong beasts,
S o dragons are amazing in every way!

Khadijah Khan (10)
Aldborough Primary School, Ilford

Dreams

D reams about looking at my wings,

R iver flowing like whipped cream,

E ventually, I grew in wisdom and became the leader of my team.

A cotton candy tree grew in my lands.

M aybe one day, my children will like me.

S omeday, this story will finish.

Eerin Zencirei (9)
Aldborough Primary School, Ilford

Fairies

In my dreams, I saw a magic flower,
My house is made of colourful candy,
I pick up the magic blue flower there,
Where fairies are pretty as a diamond.
I was shining like a blue bird.

Alexia Lourenco Atalla (9)
Aldborough Primary School, Ilford

Pirate Life

The pirates were singing, I was there
We were singing, "A pirate you shall be!"
We saw a dragon but it was friendly.

Inan Al Montatim (8)
Aldborough Primary School, Ilford

The Mansion

I suddenly teleported to the luxurious mansion, with a
crystal-blue pool.
I could practically see all.
I explored inside with my friend, excited to see where
we would spend our weekend.

There was a grand set of stairs,
Wondering if we should ascend?
We slowly climbed, our hairs standing on end.

I used my powers to turn the lights on,
Then, standing there was my waiter, Tom.
Holding a bunch of flowers!
We followed him for what felt like hours.

Until we came to a sparkling beach,
Filled with tiny people cleaning with bleach!
I saw the golden sand, and a peach appeared in my
hand!

I ate the juicy peach, thinking of taking a swim.
Suddenly there was a loud screech!
Everything began to spin and dim, I started to feel
grim.

Kyas Burrell (10)
Chantry Primary Academy, Luton

Gaming Competition

Gaming competition starts now,
And are you ready to go whip, boom and pow,
Making high records is sort of fun,
But my dream of making it is getting shot by a gun,
Back to them, back to my dream,
But full of joy is what I mean,
Adults soon start to cheer,
But I'm trying my best, so I'm drinking beer,
I want to go to first place,
But the tracks lead me, so I trace,
The round finishes, so I wait,
But food is coming, so I get a plate,
When we wait to finish the round,
Some of us are starting to bound,
As the round is still on,
But the trophy is wished,
For it is going to be gone,
The round finishes, so I wait for the results,
I won, I won, like I'm doing a vault.

Kibriyah Yaseen (9)
Chantry Primary Academy, Luton

Future

F amilies from long ago. Anyone, friend or foe, is a family who are robot agents

U can't miss out! A dream city is a choice for you and me

T ry to avoid the dark robot and agent (they shoot lightning sparks). My friends and I can't get out. We run everywhere and all about

U will never escape! Sadness and tragedy can wait! I don't feel safe

R olling is a hovercar from 'Back to the Future'. We have no choice, but the robot lost his voice

E nvious, the agent wanted this. He knew the robots wanted it, too. The crystals broke and no one spoke. We needed to find the parts before it was game over...

Marcel Kouadio (10)
Chantry Primary Academy, Luton

Who Am I?

In the mirror around daytime,
I ask myself who am I?
My mum says I'm beautiful in every way,
But my best friend states I'm a little cray cray,
I'm from Jamaica and Barbados, two hot places,
But when I am running I think I'll stick to painting

I love myself in every way possible and so should you,
But don't become a pick me, because they'll start
picking on you

Who am I? I'm Rayanne Payne,
The most unique you'll ever meet,
Despite people having the same name as me,
I'm the most unique girl you'll ever see.

Rayanne Payne (9)
Chantry Primary Academy, Luton

World War One

In my dream, every night,
I wonder if women can get rights.
One by one, getting rejected,
Praying if the jets can save us.

Feeling controlled,
Never getting chances,
In church praying,
If the jets can come and save us.

Women cleaning, men dancing,
Boom! I am in World War One,
Proving men wrong.

Saving lives left and right,
Effortlessly earning rewards,
Again and again.

Men with no choice, but to give us rights,
"Hip hip hooray," everyone yells.
Will there be peace again?

Assvina Pathmasri (10)
Chantry Primary Academy, Luton

A Calm Sight

A calm, vast night,
A brimming light shone bright,
A calm kid was in the garden,
Near the dazzling, scented flower bed,
With a brown bear called Ted,
"O, what a peaceful night," the little girl said,
Her mum brought out a warm glass of milk,
A blanket and a pillow made of silk,
A big, fluffy cloud came down,
The little girl gave a light frown,
"O, my dear Ted, always be happy,"
Said the girl, being a bit snappy,
The little girl fell asleep,
Her mum went outside to check on her
With a light creep.

Tasnim Amin (10)
Chantry Primary Academy, Luton

Our School, Our Teachers

In halls where laughter brightly rings,
Our school, where learning spreads its wings,
Teachers guide with hearts so true,
In every lesson, something for me to pursue.

From maths to art, they lead the way,
Through challenges, they help us away,
In our school's embrace, we all unite,
With teachers who inspire, and shine bright.

So here's to them, forever grand,
In our school, hand in hand,
Together we learn, and together we strive,
In the heart of learning, our spirits are alive.

Yahya Almusa (9)
Chantry Primary Academy, Luton

Night Fairies

Every night in my dreams,
I think of colours and fairies,
I stumble in the dark midst,
Lighted by dots of light,
Night fairies fly giggling around me,
They fly me to the tallest tree,
Where a little village greets me,
Destroyed like a fallen temple pillage,
The fairies weep and weep,
Worried I step back and slip,
Falling down down until I thump,
Onto my bedroom floor,
I leap in surprise and ask myself,
Have I had this dream before?
Unfortunately, I say bye to the night fairies.

Esmai Greening (9)
Chantry Primary Academy, Luton

The Scary Monster

Nothing has appeared around me,
In this strange land,
I could see doors opening,
I stepped on the floor,
Glancing left and right,
All I could see was blood on the floor,
How could I get there with blood on the floor?
Today, something appeared, creaking when I stepped,
My worst nightmare is monsters,
Creeping up to me,
Running for my life from the monster,
Early at night, I was lost,
A dragon came and helped me,
Suddenly, I woke up safe at home in bed,
I was glad I was at home.

Saleha Begum (10)
Chantry Primary Academy, Luton

28

Hot And Cold

Mysterious door on the stairs
On the other side of this mysterious planet
Led by the door
My little brother was shivering
So confused in the brightness
Warm on the other side, laboratory in the distance
No fear to be seen
Government announcement stay in your house
Not be seen
We will take care of the bot people
Don't let them get a single glimpse of you
The silence after the message got louder in his brain
Stomping came but Kenan woke up and saw that
It was all a
Dream.

Kenan Efeturk (9)
Chantry Primary Academy, Luton

Good And Evil

G ood dreams are me and you,
O ther dreams that are but all,
O ther dreams are menacing,
D ecorate your dreams with good.

A fter, don't destroy it,
N ext, don't destroy your life,
D on't do it.

E yes are blinded with evil,
'V entually you will be paralysed with it,
I f you stay good, it will not happen,
L ater you'll have a perfect life.

Samanta Tunaityte (9)
Chantry Primary Academy, Luton

The Fear Of The Unknown

Nothing in the room, but a wolf and me,
I took a step back, as nervous as can be,
I looked left and right, but still, nothing came to help me,
Ow, it bit me,
It started to chase me as fast as could be,
I felt nervous, anxious, worried and frustrated,
Could this be a dream?
I hoped this was all a joke,
It started howling, as dangerous as could be,
Suddenly, the lights went out,
The doors were locked,
And it ended as a dream.

Emre Cincik (10)
Chantry Primary Academy, Luton

Glorious Colosseum

It's time, I'm on my way through the gates,
Tartarus is closer than it ever was,
This is where the gladiators go when they die,
Thousands of Romans fill the arena,
Defeaning me with their roar,
I see the emperor, his wine as red as blood,
The sand beneath my feet is as hard as rock,
And the sun blinds me,
Terrified and excited, my destiny before me,
An honourable death is the only way I can be proud.

Leo Spinks (10)
Chantry Primary Academy, Luton

The Beach

T he beach was in front of his toes,
H e was going head first with his nose,
E veryone watched, "There he goes!"

B ut he splashed and everyone moaned,
E ven though he was having fun, it changed,
A s he turned, he saw a shark racing to him,
C limbing out the water, screaming with fear,
"H omey, there is a shark!" Nothing was there.

Jhavair Scott (10)
Chantry Primary Academy, Luton

Love And Hate

I can't believe my eyes.
Do you even realise?
All I feel is love and hate,
Then again, the world will never be great.
Before you die,
Think of a beautiful dream where you can fly.
The sun and moon make everything, even states,
Swift as wind, they'll steal your fate.
I feel empty.
If everything is destroyed, be wary.
The sun has light,
Whereas darkness is twilight.

Takudzwa Gweshe (10)
Chantry Primary Academy, Luton

Football For Life

F ootball is my life
O thers think it's bad
O utside the box, that's as sharp as a knife
T alk 'til I get mad
B ehind me were my friends
A fter that, I got food
L ater, Manchester United got a penalty
L aughter because they will lose
E ven the other team was having fun
R obbie was feeling a bit dumb.

Robbie Evans (10)
Chantry Primary Academy, Luton

Football Dreams

On a lonely pitch there I stand,
The dull and grey empty land,
Trying to fulfil my wishes and dreams,
But no one is there to redeem my dream.

I hear footsteps around my feet,
There is a voice saying, "Score a goal and you are complete,"
"Can you help me, you can score more than zero,"
The almighty goal machine Lewandowski was standing next to me.

Mila Muzyka (9)
Chantry Primary Academy, Luton

Dreams

It was a beautiful day oh so bright,
Would it stay the same I was not right,
Behind my back,
I heard a crack,
Heading to the arcade,
But little did I know it was a maze.

Hands out the ground filling me with dread,
Should I stay and fight or run from the dead?
The shrivelled hand grabbed my leg,
Falling forward I found myself in bed.

K'Treyah Davis-Henry (10)
Chantry Primary Academy, Luton

A Dream

In a world of pillows, soft and light,
Where the moon winks and the stars sigh,
Close your eyes,
It's time to play in a magical realm,
Where dreams hold and sway.

A land of candy clouds and sugary streams,
Where giggles float on vanilla ice cream,
Unicorn carousels spin with delight,
As rainbow streams are filled with delight.

Sulaiman Ibn-Zabid (9)
Chantry Primary Academy, Luton

Fortnite

F all damage is the easiest way to die!

O nly good people can win.

R eloading takes a long time.

T o be eager to win!

N ice people who aren't toxic don't emote!

I ndividuals, duos, trios and squads.

T o know bad people play no build and good play builds.

E ager to buy emotes or skins!

Muhammad Easa (9)

Chantry Primary Academy, Luton

Where Am I?

N eptune? Stars? Where am I?
E scape from the place? But I won't!
P eople think that it's a joke, but it's not.
T he future will arrive like this.
U ntil a gigantic black hole sucks the submarine in!
N o, why do I see a chicken floating?
E xit, where are you? My dream... Where am I?

Santhosh Santhirakumar (10)
Chantry Primary Academy, Luton

My Dreams

I can see the beach, long and wide,
The beautiful sea going side to side
With my friends and family
And a huge smile on my face.

The light breeze hits my face
The smile on my face is as bright as the sun
And I'm having lots of fun
And, at night, looking at the stars
And the wonderful night sky.

Thinuki Jayasingha (9)
Chantry Primary Academy, Luton

Flowers

Roses are red,
Violets are blue,
I have a dream,
You're probably having one too,
If you didn't,
What would you do?

Daisies are white,
Just like clouds,
I have a dream,
To touch the sky.

Lavender is purple,
Just like grapes,
I wish the colour,
Was used more.

Syeda Ada Batool (10)
Chantry Primary Academy, Luton

Out The Window

Just me, myself and I,
As I watch the birds go by,
Out the window, I can see,
A tiny little bumblebee!
Children playing, having fun,
Lots of space for everyone.
Out the window I can see,
People smiling with glee!
Now it's time to go eat lunch,
Hope you like this poem ever so much!

Chloe Antwi (10)
Chantry Primary Academy, Luton

Dread Wood

A depressing and dreadful school,
For 11 to 12-year-olds,
It still looks royal,
But when you see what they do you will be shocked,
Eggs for breakfast every day,
Apples for a snack,
You can't choose but the teachers do,
It is a traumatising school.

Saniyah Rafique (10)
Chantry Primary Academy, Luton

Nightmare

N o one else alive,

I n a dark house,

G uys are zombies,

H orrid nightmares,

T ragedy all night,

M any people are dead,

A nyone else alive?

R ight, just me,

E veryone, can you hear me?

Khavii Allen (9)
Chantry Primary Academy, Luton

Flying Unicorn

Outside my window, I saw a unicorn flying
I was so happy I started crying
As I reached out to see
My mum came shouting, with energy
She said, "What are you doing up so late at night?"
But then she saw the beautiful sight.

Hayrah Mahmood (9)
Chantry Primary Academy, Luton

The Cave

T ry to keep quiet
H ide and don't move a muscle
E nd up by a lake

C ut wood to make a fire
A nd fight for your life
V illains appear out of nowhere
E nter somewhere safe.

Mikail Ul-Haq (9)
Chantry Primary Academy, Luton

Crazy Cats

I was in the white abyss,
I heard meows in the mist,
Crazy cats all around,
Up in the cloud,
All the cats chased after me,
I ran nervously,
I woke up in the middle of the night,
Thinking if I was alright.

Fatima Gondal (10)
Chantry Primary Academy, Luton

Talking Clouds

I saw talking clouds,
I thought it was loud,
Looking up in the sky,
Shocked to see talking clouds coming to me,
Showing me a land of candy clouds,
And sugary streams,
Where giggles float on vanilla ice cream.

Hatija Baig (10)
Chantry Primary Academy, Luton

Super Toilet

I couldn't believe my eyes,
As I walked forward,
I saw the world's biggest toilet.
As I jumped inside, it grew legs,
It started to fly in the sky,
My pet goldfish had so much fun.

Leo Singh (10)
Chantry Primary Academy, Luton

Dreams

D ancing all night long,

R eady for the show.

E veryone is cheering,

A nd my brother gives me a bow, it's

M y time to shine,

S o, here we go.

Brian Kamau (10)
Chantry Primary Academy, Luton

Train

T rains are cool
R ails are what they run on
A rticulated buses look like one
I n the train, there are seats
N o train runs without a route.

Melvin Kanteh (9)
Chantry Primary Academy, Luton

Cloud Time

In my dreams every night,
Clouds go round and round,
And I run and run,
I am done with being chased,
You better pick the pace,
Now you are the one being chased.

James Bird (10)
Chantry Primary Academy, Luton

A Tale About A Bird In The Nest

There was a bird in a nest,
And it was the best,
Of the rest,
And it got rid of pests,
And it was named Hest,
And the bird's friend was named Rest.

Aisha Ekhlas (9)
Chantry Primary Academy, Luton

Rubik's Cube

R ubik's cube, 2x2,

U se it correctly,

B e ready,

I know how to solve it,

K eep cubing,

S peed cubes.

Gabriel Enachescu (10)
Chantry Primary Academy, Luton

Zombie Apocalypse

I last dreamed it was so scary
I was so scared
Some of my classmates were zombies
And some weren't
It was the scariest story of my life!

Lava Omer
Chantry Primary Academy, Luton

The Time Dylan Got Arrested

When I got caught flying
The cops arrested me!
Then I ran away
I got into a flying car
And flew to France.

Dylan Wallington (10)
Chantry Primary Academy, Luton

The Glowing Crystal Of The Night

As I lay in my bed at the time of night
And gazed around my bedroom with my eyes wide,
There I saw the breathtaking shimmering of different-
shaped stars like dots of glitter,
Scattered across the walls,
Which projects a soothing aura of peace and glee.
With no hesitation and a rush of excitement,
Drawing the net curtains across the window.
Staring like a painting in the gallery,
The crystal moon shone into my eyes like a lantern,
Brightening the starry, dark blue sky,
As if a dream came true.

Prycheira Foster (10)
Dairy Meadow Primary School, Southall

My Friend I See You

I see you look towards the morning dove in wonder.
I see you pointing, beaming, urging me to join you in
noticing.
I see how you laugh so easily.
Joy is never far from your precious face.
I see how much you care for our planet and everything
in it.
I see how much you crave the same love, you always
give it to the world.

I see you.

Zoha Abdul Karim (11)
Dairy Meadow Primary School, Southall

Dreams

Dreams come and go like a paper aeroplane,
Not knowing if it will fly or crash,
Hesitating to make another one like a goal,
It's like a balance scale,
Some are dreams,
While others are nightmares.

Aima Rajput (11)
Dairy Meadow Primary School, Southall

The Day I Was Pulled Under

I was walking along like a dog in a suit,
When I fell in and they pulled me under,
Wrinkled faces and spears like daggers,
They told me to die or to face a battle,
I stood in a group of them like herded cattle,
I sank to the floor, my airway closed,
I thought I was a goner, but hey, who knows?
They brought me to the surface for bravery,
Then said to save their captives to live,
I muttered the words, 'bubbles to breath',
And swam to the prison, cautious not to sink,
They stabbed me with their spears so pointy,
I needed the password to be victorious,
When I saw the captives through the window,
They snarled with their teeth so yellow,
They weren't at all mellow!
I swam over, under the dock,
Where I saw Jimmy the Jock!
I got his attention, he pulled me out,
I escaped the water goblins, finally!

Dorothy Yates (10)
East Hunsbury Primary School, Northampton

The Land Of Dreams

In the Land of Dreams,
There is a swan that has never told a lie,
A fragment of a star's twinkle,
The final echo of a night sky's cry,
The oldest lady without one wrinkle,
When you find out that love has rules,
A silence that was trapped after night falls,
The secret of how clouds get so white,
The stillness of a castle's wall,
An owl's cage that has a lock so tightly stuck in a
castle that's very tall,
A thief's silent grin as he creeps into motion,
The moment when two thoughts mix into the same
potion,
The smile of a child beaming with glee,
The flowers you find in a wonderful garden,
The whip of the sand that lives by the sea,
The oldest metal that has turned into rust,
Snowflakes settling on an oak tree,
And a gobstopper made of fairy dust.

Sophie Lah-Anyane (9)
East Hunsbury Primary School, Northampton

What We Found In The Land Of Dreams

In the Land of Dreams,
There is a swan's final breath,
A fragment of a raindrop,
The final echo from the sun's laugh,
The final gleam from a smile
When the shell cracks open,
A silence that was trapped after screaming,
The secret of why life ends so fast,
The stillness of a heart no longer beating,
A spider's web that has ensnared
A bee from the hives of a honeycomb,
A thief's final, subtle grin as he enters your nightmares,
The moment your smile turns into a frown,
The sudden grating of teeth,
Juddering to a frightening scene,
A whip of air,
The wind accompanying a sunset,
Flames curling around spectacular frowns,
Snowflakes settling on the ground,
And a gobstopper made of love!

Lexie Sloanes-Ford (8)
East Hunsbury Primary School, Northampton

A Dreamless World

Without dreams,
We'll live a life,
Deprived of a future,
Unable to thrive.

Without dreams,
We'll be lost in a barren field,
Where the stars don't gleam,
Where your imagination can't yield.

Without dreams,
We'll lose our inner fires,
Light disappearing,
As quick as a million deflating tyres.

Without dreams,
We'll lose our senses,
Trapped in a wasteland,
Confined by strong fences.

Thankfully, there's a simple cure
To permanently end this disease.
Read, write and embark on new adventures
To put your mind at ease.

So, as Doctor Suess would say,
"You're off to great places,
Today is your day!
Your mountain is waiting, so get on your way!"

Jessica Santhosh (11)
East Hunsbury Primary School, Northampton

Land Of Dreams

In the Land of Dreams,
There is a swan's final breath,
A fragment of the moon's soul,
The final echo from your mouth,
The look of your soul when someone dies
When someone's put in a grave,
A silence that was trapped after you went to jail,
The secret of how your dad died,
The stillness in a scared soul,
A spiderweb that has snared a bee
From the hives at the edge of the lakes,
A thief's subtle grin as he kills you in your dreams
The moment when you die,
The sudden grating of your body as it judders to a halt,
Into your grave,
A whip of ghostly air in the wind and an ocean wide,
Flames curling their fire on everything,
Snowflakes settling on your grave,
And a gobstopper made of souls.

Matteo Angella (9)
East Hunsbury Primary School, Northampton

What We Found In The Land Of Dreams

In the Land of Dreams,
There is a swan's final breath,
A fragment of a lightning strike,
The final echo of the sun's laugh,
The gleam from a conker,
When the shell cracks open,
A silence that was trapped after life takes over,
The secret of how a rainbow appears,
The stillness in the centre of the Earth,
A spider's web that snared,
A bear from its cave,
Which sleeps in the day,
A thief's subtle grin as it jumps into death,
The moment when dark and light smack together,
The sudden grating of rain on a rainbow,
As life turns better,
A whip of lightning hitting the rocks,
Flames curling their sparks of death,
Snowflakes settling on pine trees,
And a gobstopper made of moon dust.

Ethan Elliott (8)
East Hunsbury Primary School, Northampton

What We Found In The Land Of Dreams

In the Land of Dreams
There is a swan's final tear
A fragment of the sun's beam
The final echo of a sun's laugh
The gleam from a moon
When the shell cracks open
A silence that was trapped after sleep takes over
The secret of how the sun rises so fast
The stillness in an opal's centre
A spider's web, that has snared
A bee from the hives at the edge of the lake
A thief's subtle grin as he enters your nightmare
The moment when two ideas clash together
The sudden grating of a dog snarl
Juddering to a terrible halt
A whip of a belt hitting
In an ocean wide
Flames curling their giant trees
Snowflakes settling on frozen lakes
And a gobstopper made of melted chocolate.

Milan Protasiewicz (9)
East Hunsbury Primary School, Northampton

My Dead Halloween Escape!

It was Halloween and I was very mean, this is where my poem begins.
A group of skeletons sang a chant, as they picked my bed up.
They put me in a cave, next to a grave, I decided to save what I was going to say.
I woke up, and light struck my eyes, I was only used to the night being in my sight.
There was a door, so I opened it and I saw more.
I saw the skeletons' performance as they sang the creepy chant.
I ran and ducked behind a pumpkin and hid, I stayed silent.
I saw the sun start to rise and the sun was in my eyes.
I saw one at a time disappear and I couldn't hear the chant in my ear.
I woke up and I was in my bed, there were no skeletons, no music, no pumpkins.
And then I realised it was all just a dream.

Olivia Green (10)
East Hunsbury Primary School, Northampton

In A Dream

Long ago in a dream I had
It wasn't good, it wasn't bad
I saw a portal I went through
I met a clown who was called Lou
The portal was gone as quick as a flash
In the lake, there was a splash
All of a sudden, popcorn rained from the sky
"Take cover, take cover," is what I cried
"It's rain it's like popcorn," Lou said,
"What?" I said, Lou explained that I should go to bed
I woke up, still in that bed, but I saw globes and books
They were standing up and running around
They pulled my hair, I was so scared
But then I heard my name get called
"Lucy it's time for school"
It was my Mum, I woke up instantly
Turns out it was just a dream.

Lucy Lucan (9)
East Hunsbury Primary School, Northampton

What We Found In The Land Of Dreams

In the Land of Dreams
There is a swan's final tear
A fragment of a cloud's breath
The final echo of a bird's cheap
The gleam from a chick
When the shell cracks open
The silence that was trapped after night woke up
The secret of how the world crumbles so quickly
The stillness in a spider's sleep
A flower from the field at the corner of a river
A thief's subtle grin as she takes all your coppers
The moment when two pieces click together
The sudden grating of your life ending
To a terrible halt
A whip of sadness holding you back from the horrible days
Flames curling their evil whips
Snowflakes settling on your frozen heart
And a gobstopper made of dried-up custard.

Emily Macey (8)
East Hunsbury Primary School, Northampton

Untitled

In the Land of Dreams,
There is a swan's final speech,
A fragment of the sun's light,
The final echo of the moon's tear,
The gleam from a shell when it cracks in half,
A silence that was trapped after night-time takes over,
A secret of how stars shine so bright at night,
The stillness in your back garden at night,
A spider's web that has snared a fly flying by,
A thief's subtle grin as he sneaks into your nightmares,
The moment when two clouds stick together,
The sudden grating of a car's roar when it starts,
A whip of rain dashing on your body,
Flames curling their vicious teeth.
Snowflakes settling on the icy ground,
And a gobstopper made out of frozen glass.

Sofia Pilipciuk (9)
East Hunsbury Primary School, Northampton

My Very Own Candy World

Once upon a dream, there was a land I lived on,
With dancing sour patches and jumping bonbons.
It gave me a house I've always dreamed about,
With a toffee fence, a very big doubt.
It is made of jelly with a chocolate door,
And bouncy marshmallows for the floor.
Fizzy laces as a round bush,
And liquorice is what is lush.
I have a cookie as a plate,
And two very good mates.
I have a hat that's made out of jazzlers,
And a good best friend who is a dazzler.
A cotton candy bed,
(Which is always red).
And a chocolate night light,
With a caramel charger that likes to bike.
So this is my house I will always live in,
With everything I own just being a delicious candy bin.

Gloria M (9)
East Hunsbury Primary School, Northampton

What We Found In The Land Of Dreams

In the Land of Dreams, there is a swan's final flap,
A fragment of the sunset's dust,
The final echo of the moon's cackle,
The gleam from a rainbow's beam when the shell cracks open,
A silence that was trapped after sleep takes over,
The secret of how clouds move so quietly,
The stillness in an open door,
A spider's web that has spared a bee from the hive at the edge of the sea,
A thief's subtle grin as he enters your dreams,
The sudden grating of a car's brakes, shuddering to a halt,
A whip of glitter shooting free in the wind on an ocean, wide,
Flames curling around their home protectively,
Snowflakes settling on pine trees,
And a gobstopper made of rainbows.

Meryem Akaslan (9)
East Hunsbury Primary School, Northampton

My Dream Of The Future

When I was eight I found a love,
I stepped out on stage and felt extremely happy,
When my joy spread I felt as light as a dove,
I did it again and again and I never felt lonely.

As I did it more I knew that the stage was calling me,
The packed crowds were amazing,
Always in the final, I smiled constantly,
Whenever I left I always felt buzzing.

As I'm older now, I'm still as excited as before,
I still smile every day like the smiley face emoji,
The crowds still erupt with claps and make a bang I'm sure,
I enjoy it so much, I could act every second of every day definitely.

I never want this dream to end,
When I open my eyes I want to do it all again.

Freya Hoskins (10)
East Hunsbury Primary School, Northampton

Lost!

The park was our destination,
I turned around to carry on a conversation,
My family wasn't there,
I was worried, I was scared,
I wanted to go home,
I was confused, as confused as a new baby,
I didn't know where to go,
Someone help,
I wanted to go home,
I ran forward,
Into a dark forest,
The trees loomed over me,
I was lost,
I could go forward,
I could go backwards,
I could go left or right,
Where did I need to go?
I wanted to go home,
I decided to go forward,
Soon I saw a mesmerising light,
I followed it,
It could be my family,

It was my family,
I was so overjoyed,
I didn't know what to say.

Lucy Catling (9)
East Hunsbury Primary School, Northampton

World Cup

The atmosphere was like an erupting volcano,
As the taker stepped up and with firepower,
But the keeper saved.
The pressure was like a final exam,
It was played out wide, then to the edge of the box,
Volley goal!
The fans were electric,
Players' and fans' hearts racing like cars,
And the opposition's hearts sank like the Titanic.
Suddenly, with five minutes to go and the score one-one,
A penalty had been given,
With five minutes to go, the taker stepped up,
The ball flew into the top corner,
The crowd was bouncing,
Two-one!
Surely they'd won it now.
Finally, the whistle blew,
Celebrations went on for what felt like an eternity.

Tate McMahon (10)
East Hunsbury Primary School, Northampton

Mythical Memory Land

In a land in your mind where imagination grows
Pegasuses fly and prance around to the merry sound
Passion and courage grow on trees and bushes all
around
The waves lap at the shore, bringing memories from
long ago
And in the sky-blue ocean, calmness glows.

The sun beams down joy and smiles to all around
And little people sing and dance to the tune of
memories
Their power love, their houses mini but their hearts
huge
It is silent in the night, everyone is snuggled up tight
Dreaming of sugar plums, dragons and fairies
Love wraps around you like a warm blanket.

I know I can't stay forever but it's a dream after all,
It will stay with me forever.

Hannah Macey (10)
East Hunsbury Primary School, Northampton

A Day In Wizard Mania

Little huts spread everywhere like sprinkles on a cake,
Enchanted elves as small as mice,
Clouds dance across the sky,
Witches and wizards with warm smiles.

The trees whisper amongst themselves,
"Oh, look, a human!"
The grass glistening as bright as an emerald,
The sky is as beautiful as a diamond.

Enter one of the huts a normal human,
Exit the hut as a magical species,
Where you will learn all sorts of spells,
And impress your family and friends.

The time to leave this place has come,
You will be missed by everyone you've seen,
The portal appears, you say your last goodbyes,
You will never forget this memory.

Maya Dobranici (9)
East Hunsbury Primary School, Northampton

The Dragon Dunes

I'm far in the middle of the desert
Where all of the dragons soar
I just really want to go home...
But water I need more.

I'm scared and nervous, too
Dragons can breathe fire!
"Wait! I can see a castle!"
I can climb a spire.

I'm far in the middle of the desert
Where all the dragons soar
I just really want to go home...
Wait! I've said this before!

All the dragons, breathing fire
Soaring through the air,
One time I almost get hit
I'm truly in despair.

I hit myself on the head,
I'm standing on lots of moons,
I wake up in my bed...
I've escaped the Dragon Dunes!

Oliver Barbour (9)
East Hunsbury Primary School, Northampton

A Dream For Any Footballer

The ball is crossed in
It glides through the air
There's only one thing left to do
The team are in despair
The skill is very dangerous
But Ronaldo doesn't care
He jumps up in the air
What is he gonna do?
A volley? A header?
It could be a scorpion kick too
Ronaldo turns around
He lifts one foot
He connects with the ball
"Oh, Ronaldo, he's Real Madrid's main tool"
Zidane has hands on his head in shock
Ronaldo's just scored from a bicycle kick
He's made the stadium rock
There's tension in the stands
There's tension in the air
Surely after this goal
There's tension everywhere.

Reyes Paynton-White (11)
East Hunsbury Primary School, Northampton

The Palace Of Clouds

A cloudy palace sitting there, inviting us in,
It will wrap us in its comforting bubblewrap,
Nothing can penetrate us when we are inside,
I just can't wait to go in!

"Let's go in!" I beam,
All my friends and family are there,
The cloud palace is like unbreakable heaven,
Giving you all the best emotions.

We bounce in,
Everything we desire is here,
As the sun sets, I hear a deafening pop,
Crunch! Crash! Rip! The clouds split!

It pours down, down, down,
The sky cartwheeling as we tumble,
I gasp as I sit up on my comfortable bed,
I sigh sadly,
It was just a dream, I wish I could've stayed.

Lottie Chapman (9)
East Hunsbury Primary School, Northampton

Magical Dream Land

In my dreams, I'm in Magical Dream Land,
Where the stars glisten like diamonds in the sky,
Sequins fall down from the majestic emerald sky,
Fairies fly upon the floating fluffy clouds.

Magical Dream Land is full of magic and colours,
Mermaids dash like cats running on the grass,
The joyful fairies chattering away in the meadows,
The beautiful tasty cotton candy laughs happily,
Colourful flowers beaming from their soft beds.

Magical Dream Land is full of life and nature,
The shimmering sea is like a twinkling star at night,
The glimmering mermaids dance joyfully on the smooth sand,
Magical Dream Land is in my dreams, oh I wish it was real!

Clara Taylor (10)
East Hunsbury Primary School, Northampton

What We Found In The Land Of Dreams

In the Land of Dreams,
There is a swan's final flap,
A fragment of the last star,
The final echo of a feather falling,
The gleam of a snake when the shell cracks open.

A silence that was trapped after midnight,
The secret of how clouds move so fast,
The stillness of an opal's centre,
A spiderweb that has trapped a bee from the lake,
A thief's stubbled grin as he grabs your soul.

The moment when two ideas create another,
The sudden grating of a car's brakes juddering to a
halt,
A whip of waves on an ocean wide,
Flames curling at the wood,
Snowflakes settling on a newborn baby,
And a gobstopper made of earth.

Millie Leighton
East Hunsbury Primary School, Northampton

Dreams

Your dreams are your future,
Your dreams are your past,
Your dreams are your culture,
This dream could be your last

Imagine...

Forests as peaceful as heaven,
Melodies soft, and all is forgiven,

Or

Devil eyes glaring at you,
Bad things being compared with you.

There are many different types of dreams,
As there are many different types of trees,
There are good dreams, bad dreams, rad dreams and
sad dreams.

Don't let your imagination take control,
As this could lead to things being untold,
Sleep tight, stay in the right,
And most importantly,
Don't forget to switch off your light.

Yash Singh (11)
East Hunsbury Primary School, Northampton

86

Dreamland

In Dreamland, everything is strange,
My neighbour wears a clown shoe and a suit and tie.
Everything's weird in Dreamland,
That's something you can't change.
My teacher has a long top hat,
No one knows why.
When I wake up,
My bed kicks me out.
When I eat breakfast,
My spoon hits a jig.
I say good day to my mother,
Who grows a snout.
I take my pet to school,
It's a pig!
When I brush my teeth,
I use cherry juice.
I read my book about fish,
Snuggled up to my pet moose.
I soon wake up to my favourite dish.
That is my Dreamland (quite a weird one),
But... it sure is fun!

Poppy Cook (9)
East Hunsbury Primary School, Northampton

Today I Rode A Bike To The Moon

Have you ever rode a bike?
Have you been to the moon?
Have you ever rode a bike to the moon?
Well... I have and if you ever do, look out for a few things

When I was on the bike it blasted off
And went roaring in the air and shot me on my way

I saw the moon as grey as a storm
When I hopped off the bike, the moon was so sticky
It felt like a lollipop in my hair

I think I saw the sun blink and Mars wave at me
And ooh yes, I think Earth was dancing... how strange!

I think the moon is made of carrot cake
And has an ice cream flag
And gummy bears as aliens shimmying their bums.

Millie Kremenskas (7)
East Hunsbury Primary School, Northampton

Paradise Life

You close your eyes and fall asleep,
And wake up in a dream so deep,
Pink mist fills the air,
And sparkling stars fills your hair.

Tiny houses can be seen and,
Tiny people wave at you,
Purple water drips from the sky,
As you realise this is a land where people don't die.

When sparkling fireworks go boom,
Joy fills the whole entire room,
But it's not a room because...
It's paradise!

And because it's paradise,
Everything is so fluffy and nice,
But don't forget this is a dream,
So wake up as you row your boat down the stream.

Laura M (11)
East Hunsbury Primary School, Northampton

Cloud World

In a land far away,
Stands a world with excitement,
A place where you can just lie around all day,
It will really fill you with amazement.

The floor is clouds made of cotton candy,
The creatures are like loyal dogs,
This place is fun, don't be a dandy,
They have benches made of carved logs.

The houses sway in the minty wind,
They are made of chocolate sponge cake,
Here, nothing ever will be binned,
You can get free food, no need to bake.

The clouds are like bunnies, you'll laugh all day long,
This dream will sadly end with a *bong!*

Thomas Barley (9)
East Hunsbury Primary School, Northampton

So-Called Dreams

You just want to close your eyes,
But the shadows jump right out at you,
You just want to get some sleep,
But somebody is now there for you.

When you think they're gone you have a snooze,
And pray for a peaceful dream,
But the universe doesn't like you,
So a guest comes to sit.

A spider runs up your leg,
And then a ghost comes to say hello,
The shark from Jaws will now bite,
Your trypophobia kicks in.

Falling into a world of horror,
Some dreams are real,
Some are not,
But always remember to turn the lights off.

Eadie Keeley
East Hunsbury Primary School, Northampton

Life's Desire

I was abandoned when the moon glows,
In one semi-circle,
I have crossed many horizons,
Until I found something fascinating!
A portal emerged, I saw it with my eyes,
As soon as I went through, I thought I was in love,
There were wishes and glitter and many desires,
But loads of evil things can cling to you in a day!
There are potions and cauldrons that can turn you into stew,
And sweeties and candies that can make you levitate,
Come and eat and levitate and make your dreams come true,
We've got everything your mind goes on and everyone's desires!

Amelia Aran (10)
East Hunsbury Primary School, Northampton

The Monster

The crimson-red sky illuminates
the crystal-blue monster
that hits me hard, like a car hitting me.
The floor is freezing cold like one million ice cubes
squashed together.
Every time I touch the box,
it hits me like a flash.
Everyone sees it, but no one helps me.
The floor sucks me like a hoover and dust.
It always says,
"I have no intention of hurting you."
But it always does.
Every time it happens,
the ice cracks and I fall in.
Its eyes are green like an emerald.
The worst bit of it all is that it's in Paris.

Zachary Boodhoo (9)
East Hunsbury Primary School, Northampton

The GOAT ~ Bellingham

There's me watching football every night,
Proud to be watching it; it is so nice.
Playing and watching is my thing,
Striking and scoring that is so me.

My favourite player is Bellingham, so you see,
He's nice; he's cool, and he is my idol.
He makes the best defenders look bad,
He likes going mad.

He is the top man,
He's never been sad,
As he is the top man,
He makes Ronaldo look bad.

Let's just put it there: he is the GOAT,
At twenty years of age,
And he's already there.

Blake Coote (9)
East Hunsbury Primary School, Northampton

94

Bread

The loaf was full of flavour, like a delicious smoothie,
The dough was being cooked like a fresh egg.
The baker made a hot, crispy croissant,
But the baker dropped it on his dirty leg.

The dough was covered in powder, which was like flour,
The bread jumped out of the chrome toaster.
The loaf was as brown as a chocolate bar,
The dough was as loud as a farmer's rooster.

The bakery looked warm,
Smelt fresh, and was full of bread,
But the baker cooked so much,
His hands looked like they were dead.

Hayyan Sardar (10)
East Hunsbury Primary School, Northampton

Beast In The Dark

In a place called New York City
A little boy was born
And his name was Timmy
A scary monster he had drawn.

One night when he went to bed
There was a noise below
There was a statue of dread
A monster was on show.

It had sharp teeth and big eyes
Then it smashed through the glass
And suddenly Timmy heard a cry
As it crashed onto the grass.

The monster was about to attack
Nobody ever spoke
It was about to have a snack
But then, Timmy woke.

Harrison Balneaves (10)
East Hunsbury Primary School, Northampton

Dreamland

In Dreamland, all dreams can come true
Wish for anything, even a zoo
Or a giraffe doing jumping jacks
But one man said, I want a mansion, it's my passion

As he saw his mansion
He knew it was his fashion and passion

My house is made of money, gold and silver
As it lights up the sky almost at night
What a fright for night

As he went to bed, he bumped his head

In the morning, it's quite boring when you stop
dreaming
And wait to dream again.

Joshua Whitnall (9)
East Hunsbury Primary School, Northampton

Sweet Land

It's early in the morning in Dreamland with lots of
sweets
This is a place with lots of treats

My home is made of chocolate, all over the floor
With rainbow sprinkles, Haribo roof tiles and a hard
toffee door

The sun runs around like a hand and a clock
The moon goes dark and it locks

His smooth dark hair is like chocolate
As they walked into a sweet shop their mouths
dropped

Her hands are as soft as cotton candy
The rain bangs on the Haribo tiles.

Aliyah-Mae Kelly (10)
East Hunsbury Primary School, Northampton

Hell!

I opened my eyes to a blazing carpet of fire,
The heat was as hot as the sun,
The lava slowly staggered and crawled towards me,
I was stuck,
Strapped to big and heavy chains,
People were screaming, the lava must have got to them,
The lava called out to me,
Sizzle, sizzle,
A man was standing slurping lava into his dry mouth,
He had long black horns like death,
My mouth was as dry as a desert,
All hope was lost as my body went sizzle.

Hell!

Morgan Cosford (10)
East Hunsbury Primary School, Northampton

The Portal

To live in a cottage near a forest full of trees
We live a life full of fresh breeze
A portal we found in a valley
We went in and we were nowhere to be
All we could see was a river full of galaxy stars which
we could float on
Up ahead I saw a house made of stars of the galaxy
and crystals of the ancient gods
Our brains left us the moment we saw the house
Bang!
We opened our eyes to another portal
All we knew was it was a new mystery if we went in
there.

Carolyn Juan Anil (9)
East Hunsbury Primary School, Northampton

The Man

Raging through the door,
Drips of blood fall,
Slurps of his drink,
Form a pool of murkiness,
And the bang of the staircase alerts him.
My candlelight whispers like the demons,
And argues with me.
The opaque waters drip through the roof,
And the floorboards creak as the man approaches me.
He snatches a soda out from the fridge,
And when he opens it,
It makes a big fizz.
He throws the blankets off the beds,
And goes outside to smash the shed.

Jessica Irons (11)
East Hunsbury Primary School, Northampton

Ice Cream

Ice cream filled my mouth with exotic flavour,
As if it was my one and only saviour,
The one and only precious smell,
The one that I could never tell,
It was as if it was made from the heavens,
The heavens jumped down and cheered hooray,
As the ice cream was celebrated for a full day,
Until the ice cream screamed in fear,
As the exotic flavour was no longer here,
The people shouted and screamed,
Blankness filled the air,
Until no one was there.

Victor Puscausu (11)
East Hunsbury Primary School, Northampton

Sleeping Dreams

Dreams, dreams, amazing dreams.
They fill up your mind like a water fountain.

Clouds circle around you,
Cats cuddle close by you,
They purr to make you feel calm.

Eyes closed,
Body rests,
And dreams pop up in your head.

There are many types of dreams,
And every dream is represented by a tree.

Water drips down in joy,
Rest with peace and wake up with joy.

Dreams, dreams, amazing dreams.

Madalina Turculet (10)
East Hunsbury Primary School, Northampton

The Haunted House

The haunted house, as scary as walking alone in a
forest
The haunted house petrifying like a growling bear
The haunted house is damp and dark and will haunt
you in your dreams if you take a step inside
The floor shattered beneath his eyes
The door creaked open
As soon as he walked in the door slammed shut
The huge, grey clouds fought against the rain and hail
And if you come across a haunted house beware
Beware of the old man's fair.

Jansen Thompson (8)
East Hunsbury Primary School, Northampton

Ducks!

Ducks are small and tall and people know how funny
ducks can be,
They are as talented as can be.
Everyone gather round and plea,
For the ducks' show and then they will flee.

Ducks have a fiery temper when they are mad,
And people think that they are bad.
It could only be a duck flying through the trees.

Ducks come in all shapes and sizes,
For those who don't know,
It's the best living thing in the world.

Tatum Bradshaw (10)
East Hunsbury Primary School, Northampton

Bread

I dreamt about bread,
The bread was nutritious,
The bread was delicious,
The bread tasted like Heaven,
It was amazing.
The bread was scrumptious,
Then I dreamed about more bread,
But this time, the bread went:
Sploosh, splash, crash, pow!
It was sick,
It was cool,
It was nearly as cool as having a pool.
Then the bread played football
And then basketball,
I hope you enjoyed my poem, thank you!

Ollie Bradshaw (10)
East Hunsbury Primary School, Northampton

Rice

Rice is nice,
It's as white as snow,
And it glows in the flow,
It's nice in a bowl but not on a plate,
But either one it'll always be great.
I could be the rice crying,
Calling my name,
It'll never taste bad
And you'll never be sad!
You could hear the rice sizzle, it was ready for
preparation,
And it tasted like a sensation.
The rice danced through the air like an angel,
It was beautiful.

Shea Chambers (10)
East Hunsbury Primary School, Northampton

Once Upon A Dream

I dream about a Jeff Bezos,
Jumping in the summer breeze,
Alfie's house is a million storeys tall,
With cookie dough windows,
Pizza doors and cheese walls.

The oil dripped on the rocket,
Then the rocket took off and flew up to the moon.
The start of a new chapter.

Then the monster tried to eat me and Jedd,
The monster missed but then there were more
monsters,
Who tried to kill the rest.

Alfie Clark (9)
East Hunsbury Primary School, Northampton

Sugar Land!

A chocolate river ready to be licked,
Lollipop flowers always being picked,
A gingerbread family is always having fun,
Some bonbons are disguised as magical plums,
Cotton candy trees are proudly standing,
Strawberry lace vines are happily hanging,
Popping candy falls from the sky,
Oh my gosh, my teeth are just getting by,
I'm definitely going to get decay,
But I'm sure I'm going to be okay!

Milly Webb (10)
East Hunsbury Primary School, Northampton

Dream Horse

In a dream once before,
Horses fly around the world.
They laugh and play whilst children sleep,
Their colourful beams spread through their wreaths.

They fly and twirl with sparkly manes,
They come to Earth to entertain.
They live on a planet far and beyond,
One by one they pass the sky and I think,
They are ready to say goodbye.
With that said they left with hay,
Hope they come back again.

Erika Maria Ursu (9)
East Hunsbury Primary School, Northampton

Professional Figure Skater

Being a professional figure skater
Brings spins and turns, jumps and falls
No matter what happens
You tried after all
Skates slide by
Like sharpened knives
The crackling sounds
Make you feel alright
The light of the ice
The touch of your friend
The feeling of freedom
The feeling of life
Step on the ice
And slip and slide
The laughter of ice
Makes you wobble and glide.

Chloe Sayers (10)
East Hunsbury Primary School, Northampton

Candy Land

In Candy Land, the sky is as blue as bubblegum
The clouds are as soft as cotton candy.

In Candy Land, my house is made of gingerbread
With chocolate cement, Haribo roof tiles and a caramel
door.

In Candy Land when you step on the popping candy
rocks
It makes a big bang.

Also, the candy canes stand tall like a skyscraper
When I woke up I missed the sweets
I wish I could go back.

James Kimber (10)
East Hunsbury Primary School, Northampton

The Wizard And The Fairies

Once upon a dream, in a place so big, so true,
There are two lands that await you,
And those two beautiful worlds are full of wizards,
Fairies, unicorns, royalty and superpowers.

One day a wizard appeared and tried to cast a spell on
the fairy world,
But little did she know this place was way too powerful
for wizardry,
The unicorns were flying, trying to stop the wizard from
doing anything mysterious.

Scarlett Stockman (9)
East Hunsbury Primary School, Northampton

Untitled

The deep blue sea running towards me,
And the waves could swallow the Titanic,
The darkness could swallow my soul,
The veins carrying my blood became blue,
Everything was becoming blurry,
Everything became dark.
No longer calm,
No longer peaceful,
My body started to suffocate,
I slowly fell,
The soul that I owned fell to the bottom of the sea,
The rest is unknown to the rest of us.

Lillian Ibeh (11)
East Hunsbury Primary School, Northampton

The Ocean

I woke in the middle of the ocean, cold and terrified,
The waves loomed over, suffocating me like a black
boa constrictor,
The thunder roared like chaos, bursting my vulnerable
eardrums,
The water was absorbed into my pale body as I tried to
stay alive,
The water evaporated into the mystery fog,
The rain dripped, lightning banged and the ocean
slurped the dead creatures within,
I woke up in a nightmare.

Milly Benson (11)
East Hunsbury Primary School, Northampton

Sweet Sparkly Magical Autumn

Her soft, sweet, sparkly bedroom was white, blue and gold
The top was covered in sweets
It seemed like a tropical dream
Knock, knock!
"Who are you?"
"Come join me!" said the sweets
"Please, I don't bite!"
"Fine, but let me show you something
My personality is happy as the sun!"
She ran with excitement
She was hidden in the night.

Daisy Gericke (8)
East Hunsbury Primary School, Northampton

Football

The crowd was erupting like a volcano,
Seeing flashing lights beaming down on me.
The pressure was intense,
He could be the hero or the villain.
He thought for a moment, he struck the ball,
As sweet as a candy cane,
And it buckled into the top corner of the goal.
The opposition fell to the floor as if they passed out,
My team charged towards me as I ran to my
supporters and celebrated.

Mikey Ayub
East Hunsbury Primary School, Northampton

The Magical Land Of Dreams

This dream is as magical as a unicorn
When the dragon rolled down the hill he went ding, dang, dong
Suddenly the gummy bears spoke!
My house is as bright as the sun
When you go through the door you turn into a fairy
Look at the moon it's smiling with joy
My house is full of fairies, unicorns and all mythical creatures
Even cute bear cubs
My house is a house of fairy-tale dreams.

Ava Wild (8)
East Hunsbury Primary School, Northampton

Penalty

The penalty was as soft as,
In fact it was actually a dive.
Nothing could be done as VAR wasn't there.
The Watford fans thought their team would be left in despair.
Their promotion would be ended.
All their dreams would be shredded.
Whatever will they do...?
And here we go, the player went to shoot...

"The Leicester player stepped up for the pen."

Jason Wright (10)
East Hunsbury Primary School, Northampton

The North Sea

The waves were as strong as lightning,
The waves crashed over the island,
Sea creatures wailed beneath the thunder and rain.
As I saw the island emerging from the water,
The lightning hid in the sea.
I saw cruise ships crashing into icebergs
And sailboats ripped to pieces.
Lightning crashed, water rippled and thunder growled.
In the North Sea, no one came out alive.

Lexi Greenwood-Walden (11)
East Hunsbury Primary School, Northampton

Falling

I dream about falling
Falling slow as a snail
The freezing cold welcoming me in
I feel I could freeze and die
I'm starting to panic
Tears are filling my eyes
The blood-red moon is getting small
That can only mean one thing after all
The fluffy clouds turning red
Blood gushing down
I scream in pain
Thump!
Maybe this was all a game...

Inna Monita (10)
East Hunsbury Primary School, Northampton

Sleep And Dream

Close your eyes and sleep,
Don't wake up from a deep sleep,
Float away and drift,
Watch your body go up like a lift.

Sleep is the one thing people need,
There's no need for speed,
In a deep dream,
There's no one mean (mostly).

In Dreamland just dream,
Let the birds talk as much as you,
Bye for now,
See you another time.

Matilda Barr (11)
East Hunsbury Primary School, Northampton

122

The Lion

As it slumped out of the cave,
It raised its head all mighty and brave,
All you could see was a glorious creature,
Rising up with a fascinating feature,
Its mane like the sun,
As it went out on a morning run,
A prowl and a growl and a defining roar!
He was out and hunting once more,
All the trees and bushes too,
Bowed down to the one true,
The lion.

Henry Elliot (10)
East Hunsbury Primary School, Northampton

The North Sea

The waves were screaming
Like a child who lost a loved one
As the sea creatures below tried to eat my raft
I fell into the sea
Stuck in a dream
Lost at sea.

Then... *Bang!*
A boat hit an iceberg
People fell into the deep, dark, cold water
With my last breath leaving
As everything had gone dark
Stuck in a dream
Lost at sea.

Mia Kremenskaite (10)
East Hunsbury Primary School, Northampton

The Flight Of Death

The sky rumbled; my throat bubbled as a strike of lightning hit the plane.

The fear, the rain, the screaming, the pain.

What a tragedy, so frightening! Fire lashed, people crashed.

Rumours have been made; I don't know what I gained.

Lesson learned: don't fly a random plane.

Oh, the flight of death, the flight of death.

Daniel Dawodu (10)
East Hunsbury Primary School, Northampton

Above The Clouds

The clouds are as soft as a blanket
The wonderful, sweet clouds white as snow
A sweet cloud was as soft as a bed
Puffy purple cotton candy mixing
Soft, pink, sweet dust poofed around the sky
Moving past spinning the stars
The peaceful clouds yawned and separated
Birds chirped at my feet
I stared at the gorgeous view
Sad clouds cried.

Isla Husbands (8)
East Hunsbury Primary School, Northampton

The Beach

As the aqua-blue waves crashed against the glistening rocks,
The vivid orange morning roamed the sky,
The emerald-green leaves that swayed at the top of the shining palm trees,
Danced and swooshed along the morning sky,
As night rose, the stars shone like glazing lightbulbs,
The beige sand lay along the beach,
With pale shells sitting along.

Castalella Zarzuela-Newey (10)
East Hunsbury Primary School, Northampton

The Animal Abduction

I dream about animals abducting my living room,
Like the wave that swallowed the Titanic,
Tigers teaming with panthers, and lions joining forces,
The fluff of the couch reaches my feet,
Torn apart into smithereens,
Drip, drip, drip,
The sound of the dogs drooling on the floor,
The rug screams with pain, wrath and sorrow.

George Mantelis (10)
East Hunsbury Primary School, Northampton

A Magical Land

It started when the cupcakes fell to the castle floor,
Within a magical land that was as magic as the fair,
And as mythical as unicorns flying through the air.
When the castle was full of cupcakes,
They fell in a blink of an eye, *bong, splat!*
The cupcakes then shimmered in the light, as they
twinkled like the stars.

Sophie Trigg (7)
East Hunsbury Primary School, Northampton

The Haunted House

The rain dripped down
The rain got faster
The trees waved like flags
It was midnight
Darkness!
He touched his ear
And felt no fear
He saw a camera in the middle of the room
And saw a witch sitting on a broom
Now for him there was no place to hide
And the witch took him on a broomstick ride.

Ezekiel Gill (8)
East Hunsbury Primary School, Northampton

Eyes Of Darkness

A sound like a bomb enveloped the house,
The stairs looked as if they led into the depths of Hell.
Blood crept under the door,
A killer had struck.

The scream was like a child's cry,
A yell in the starry sky.
And, when the screaming finally died,
All I saw were dark, black eyes.

Oliver Clements-Hill (11)
East Hunsbury Primary School, Northampton

Dragon Apocalypse

This morning I woke up only to see out of my window a
dragon,
I ran all around the house, but no one was there,
The sun was rising as fast as Bruce Lee's kicks,
I went outside and all I could hear was roaring from
ear to ear,
I got warned about my surroundings,
But I got swooped and gobbled up.

Louix Faulkner (9)
East Hunsbury Primary School, Northampton

The Dark Closes In

I live in a cottage in the woods,
Come and visit me for a surprise.
The door creaks open
When the moonlight screams,
The spider zooms to shut the door.

My ghosts suck you into a ditch:
You scream.
You *bang*, *crash*, and *bash*,
No one comes to help.

Sophie Elkington (8)
East Hunsbury Primary School, Northampton

The Haunted Castle

Beware, beware, the castle up there it's very, very
haunted.
A girl went up there one day and disappeared in
seconds.
Where, where did she go?
We have never seen her since.
Maybe a monster ate her there,
And she's now in his rum tum tum,
Weeping with a broken heart.

Millie Parsonson (7)
East Hunsbury Primary School, Northampton

Stranded At Sea

The wind screamed like a banshee,
As the waves aggressively crashed like glass.
I glanced at the lightning,
That shattered a black cloud,
Which consumed all of my happiness.

I was stranded at sea,
I was lonely.
There was no sign for help.

Sophie Godwin (10)
East Hunsbury Primary School, Northampton

The Sports Car

The sports car was in my way,
The sports car said,
"I'm not in your way."
"Yes, you are!" said the tiger.
"But Tiger, you are in my way now!"
But the tiger had a bucket in his den,
And the sports car lost his mirror.

David Pasere (7)
East Hunsbury Primary School, Northampton

The Nightmare

Wind screaming unable to escape the nightmare,
As cold as ice, as scary as a saw,
As loud as a roar.
People screaming as they run down the jet-black night.
Torture, torture.
Trapped in this horrible nightmare,
Trapped in a cage unable to be saved.

Ella Stonhill (10)
East Hunsbury Primary School, Northampton

A Unicorn When I Get Home

A unicorn is waiting for me at home
Is she high or is she low?
Is she left or is she right?
She crashes into the wall with a flash and a bang!
The sun shimmers and glows and flickers sparks of
happiness in the sky
My unicorn is waiting for me at home.

Charlotte Irons (8)
East Hunsbury Primary School, Northampton

The Door Of Secrets

All you could see was a door at the end of the hallway.
Blood dripped down from the ceiling.
The room was as quiet as space.
You could see eyes following you as you crept forward.
But, as soon as you got to the end...
The door revealed its secrets.

Noah Pickering (11)
East Hunsbury Primary School, Northampton

All Alone

Trees were staring silently,
The sun turned into the moon,
The wind danced like a ballerina girl,
The dark green grass was a green watermelon,
The dull brown mud was the girl,
The girl was sad,
She heard something
Something had happened.

Victoria Cegolea (10)
East Hunsbury Primary School, Northampton

The Dough

The dough was a toffee, coffee madness.
The dough was a forming cloud shimmering with the sun.
The dough hung in the oven like a war was ahead.
The morning sun awakened them to their brand-new self.
The dough was alive and welcomed to its new home.

Charlie Maddison (10)
East Hunsbury Primary School, Northampton

That Living Thing

Once in a dream, there was a box
Inside the box, I saw that living thing
It was black and then its eyes opened
It chased me for miles and miles
And then it all turned white
The black stopped because it got me
I woke up...

Mason Kremenskas (9)
East Hunsbury Primary School, Northampton

My Dream

I wanna be like Seaman,
The crowd chanting my name,
The crowd erupted as the composed penalty stepped up,
And Ratcliffe saved!
The atmosphere exploded,
Rebound top,
But hang on, Ratcliffe's hand swiped it over.

Charlie Ratcliffe (11)
East Hunsbury Primary School, Northampton

Bing, Bang, Boom

Bing, bang, boom! What's that sound?
Bing, bang, boom! There's something in the gloom.
Bing, bang, boom! Is it a baboon?
Bing, bang, boom! It's somewhere in the room.
Bing, bang, boom! It's in this very room.

Thomas Barbour (10)
East Hunsbury Primary School, Northampton

My Castle

My castle is as light as a cloud
My castle is as delightful as a duck
My castle is always clean and never has any muck

There's a penguin on my bed
There's a platypus on my head
I'm going to my shed.

Olivia Kelly (8)
East Hunsbury Primary School, Northampton

When I Touched The Sun

When I touched the sun,
I felt like my worries were done,
When I touched the sun,
I felt like my life had been spun,
When I touched it, it let my dreams run wild,
And maybe, just this once,
I could be free.

Ryley Jwanczuk (10)
East Hunsbury Primary School, Northampton

Imagination World

In a world far away,
A club you will see,
TV everywhere and free stay,
Unicorns, dragons and fairies,
You will have the time of your life,
You will have friends and family,
Go crazy and have fun.

Emily Griffiths (9)
East Hunsbury Primary School, Northampton

The Mystery Of The Missing Brother

Where's my brother?
Here or there?
Has he gone through the window?
Or through the door?
Where is my brother?
Can it be true?

Luisa Matayoshi Marchesin (7)
East Hunsbury Primary School, Northampton

Phoenix

I go to sleep and see a land with my favourite people
The one with the lightning bolt zap on his head, Harry
Potter
The one who is funny, Ron Weasley
And not their mate, but their true friend, Hermione
Granger
They seem a little curious so we have a little adventure
Suddenly, we see underwater
There's a mystical land shaped like a phoenix
Feathers so hot they light up the ocean's features
I fall, scream and land on a phoenix's back
It gives me a little nudge and then we fly off
I feel excited, but then I wake up, feeling like it was real
With a spark, the very next night, I dream the same
dream
I suddenly remember I was flying around
I feel the heat and the cosy warmth around
I belong here, I don't want to go, but my friends are
shouting
"Come on, let's go!"
We all walk off but my phoenix stays close by
And every other night, I jump up high, high, high!

Skye James (9)
Gladestry Church-In-Wales Primary School, Kington

I Had A Dream

In the place of my dream, it is all ponies, ponies, ponies,
The rolling hills lead down to a babbling brook,
Where the ponies use the trees as a shady nook,
I see pretty piebalds showing like no pony in the world,
Strawberry roans and blueberry roans race to be best,
Dapple greys crunching on their apples,
Ponies drinking their coffee, which I hear is the best,
Dressage horses' shiny hooves showing extravagant
moves,
In the middle of the day, I leave out the hay,
For the foals, to let them play,
Horses small or tall always want to roll,
Up in the sky, the red kites fly,
The ponies realise it is dinner time and walk up the field
in a big long line,
A Shetland pony short and sweet, surely he likes to eat,
With the setting sun, the thoroughbreds like to run.

Nia Price (10)
Gladestry Church-In-Wales Primary School, Kington

Gone Down The Trapdoor

G one! I'm gone down the trapdoor into the lost of the lost, stuck up in this sticky swamp, Help, oh, help, get me out, I'm not old like a grandpa, I'm new. How did my owner lose me already on this day?

O nly old toys live in this place, oh no, I made a mistake, I have to go now.

N one of these broken toys are like us, no they're different to us, they're not the same at all, let's go and see some more around this place.

E verything is gone down here if they're broken they go down here through the trapdoor, don't worry, you'll get used to it, bye, see you next year, I hope so.

Meredith Robinson
Gladestry Church-In-Wales Primary School, Kington

Dreamland

D riving up a field in a dripping mud tractor to feed magical sheep.

R unning away from a sparkling tup so fierce it looks like it is about to kill me.

E ntering the tractor after unravelling the net off the magic bales.

A fter a hard working day, we go in the warm house for a cuppa.

M y grandad has a sleep after watching the magic TV.

L iving the life after we wake up to a magical sunrise.

A mazing cows wake up with a magical moo.

N aughty sheep wait at the sparkling silver gate to be fed.

D ogs are farmers' best friends that never leave them alone.

Albie Jones (10)
Gladestry Church-In-Wales Primary School, Kington

The Nightmare

N obody told us that we'd be here

I told the orange wizard and we shuddered in fear

G oats all around us had big bulging eyes and sharp, sabre teeth

H elping their terrible habit of eating rabbit pies

T urning to the left, I thought I'd see a wee goat but

M assive mammoths were guarding a fort

A nd those ice age giants looked like they'd been fought

R eady to spring past those massive monsters I realised they were multiplying

E ver since then, I've been scared to go to bed.

Wyn Daman Thomas (8)
Gladestry Church-In-Wales Primary School, Kington

Luke

L ovely inch-perfect darts as the commentator shouts 180 all day!

I nfant on the world stage shocking everyone.

T esting world champions who have won multiple world titles.

T he kid who is going to be part of the amazing next generation,

L eaving his opponents speechless as he hits nine darters every game.

E verlasting wins he can't stop being unstoppable as his darts twist and turn towards the dartboard.

R ich after winning £200,000 leaves his opponent crying and weeping as he shocks.

Cian Tolley (10)
Gladestry Church-In-Wales Primary School, Kington

Mo Salah

M o Salah is the top goal scorer, as fans cheer all day long for him,

O nce winning the Golden Boot for most goals scored.

S uddenly, Mo Salah scores a hat-trick to make a comeback to win,

A im, fire! Mo Salah scores every shot he takes, even out of the box,

L ong shot every game, including nail-biting derbies, he always finds the net,

A fter most games he goes to collect his amazing 'Man of the Match' award,

H ome at Anfield, he's at his best forever, whenever.

Tom James (10)
Gladestry Church-In-Wales Primary School, Kington

When I Lay My Head Down

When I lay my head down and close my eyes,
I see stars, Mum, Dad and Poppy sitting on the edge of
a mountain,
Looking at the stars.

When I lay my head down and close my eyes,
I float up to my mum, dad and Poppy,
I feel like a star,
We float above in the sky with fairies flying by.

When I lay my head down and close my eyes,
I'm gliding with my family,
We go back down to the glorious ground,
To have a picnic and watch the dinosaurs go by
perfectly to the ground.

Rowan Vincent (9)
Gladestry Church-In-Wales Primary School, Kington

Untitled

F ierce footballers are flying across the football pitch

O ut comes Harry Kane in comes Timo Werner

O nly white kits are allowed on this pitch

T he long field with players running up and down

B alls are flying everywhere in practice

A nge Postecoglou shouting at the players to get back and defend

L iverpool lost to Tottenham 2-1 at the Hotspurs stadium

L ads loudly loving Son as he strikes the ball into the back of the net.

Daniel Lloyd (11)
Gladestry Church-In-Wales Primary School, Kington

A Special Stare

An arena with soft and fluffy ground,
Metal roof all safe and sound,
All you hear are hooves on the cake-like sand.
Clip-clop, clip-clop as he trots along the line,
I feel free and let myself go...
I fall off with a thud.
Broken bone? I don't know!
Get back on for someone is there to comfort me.
After the big fall, I feel well looked after,
Before I know it, CD is there,
Before my eyes with his comforting stare.

Lyra Parry (9)
Gladestry Church-In-Wales Primary School, Kington

The Magical Land Of Dancing Animals

I had a dream where magical things began
Unbelievably bright birds fly and play
Crazy colourful cows with cream-coloured hooves
creep around my house
Seashell sheep with cotton candy coats leaping lazily
like leopards
Come out at midnight, and at two o'clock, they
disappear
Sometimes I leave some sweet treats but they don't
eat them
They turn them into a potion and leave it for me
I don't know where I am
I want to get out.

Sofia Hodge (10)
Gladestry Church-In-Wales Primary School, Kington

In My Dreams

Day turns to night,
My dreams take flight,
I see him there,
An amazing dapple grey pony,
Amazing hooves beating the ground.

Day turns to night,
My dreams take flight,
Fluorescent rainbows,
Float in the sky,
Clouds dance between them.

Day turns to night,
My dreams take flight,
I sit drinking sparkling river water,
Glistening glass windows,
And soft comfy cushions.

Lili Davies (10)
Gladestry Church-In-Wales Primary School, Kington

Scared

In my magical dream
I was in Australia at the big high park
In my magical dream
Climbing to the highest piece of equipment
In my magical dream
I got to the top and had a meltdown
In my magical dream
My parents heard me
In my magical dream
They needed to get me and save me
In my magical dream
They saved me and I was fine
In my magical dream
My little brother did... nothing.

Eli Knight (8)
Gladestry Church-In-Wales Primary School, Kington

A Different World

When I am older I hope bears, wolves and other
animals are free and safe
When I am a grown-up, I will live in a forest in Vietnam
When I am older, I hope there will be no rubbish in the
sea
If I had power, my power would be to blow up the
world and start again maybe with TV
I hope animals will be safe
I hope the trees won't be cut down
I hope people will not drive as much.

Florence Jauncey-Wellard (8)
Gladestry Church-In-Wales Primary School, Kington

Forest

F rom my bed to the field, with my friend Charlie scared to death,

O n that night I had a fright with trees that creaked without leaves, I was very, very scared,

R unning away from cats and bats and ran scaring, daring,

E xtreme scares, more scorpions and spiders,

S eriously, I hate rats and I hate scary cats,

T erribly trembling, running away.

Wilbur Fraser (7)
Gladestry Church-In-Wales Primary School, Kington

Luke Littler

L ittler is the next Great Of All Time.

I t is 180 and triple-eight over and over again.

T he sixteen-year-old wins over and over.

T he kebab legend.

L ittler is insane.

E very player is losing against him apart from Humphries, maybe next year.

R apid darts hit 180 for Luke Littler.

Huw Stafford Tolley (10)
Gladestry Church-In-Wales Primary School, Kington

Football

F ierce football players surrounding me

O range T-shirts are all I can see

O wazi FC do not like me

T ense I fell

B ack I went until I bumped with Neymar

A ll the people look at me

L ionel Messi whispered to me

L ittle boy do not be scared, do not be scared.

Callum Price (8)
Gladestry Church-In-Wales Primary School, Kington

Lost

L ost in the scary world, I see glowing eyes - it could be anything.

O riginal world, it could be anything.

S ee the monster, it's a dragon! What's it doing?

T errified, I run! I'm doing it, I close my eyes... and wake at home, safe at home.

Ben James (7)
Gladestry Church-In-Wales Primary School, Kington

Lost In My Dream

In my dream dinosaurs are loose like cannonballs
With my dragons we watch dinosaurs destroy woods
Finding dinosaurs having a battle
Never expecting such a fright
Sun has risen nice and bright
Battle's over, sun has risen
Hybrid is the new Jungle King.

Teddy James (8)
Gladestry Church-In-Wales Primary School, Kington

The Dance

One day, a girl with a smile that smiled so bright,
Walked into a wood so free and bright
The clock struck nine and the lights went off,
The wood was empty and the town was lost.
The girl went further and further into the forest,
And put a fort up and started dancing.
The dance was graceful and made her smile,
It carried on for ages and for long went on.
She felt very free, not thinking of time,
The clock struck ten, but she didn't mind.
The clock struck midnight and then kept going up,
She got a bit tired but kept going on.
She ended the dance with a perfect bow,
And then went inside and cuddled in bed.

Lacey Louise (10)
Plymtree CE Primary School, Plymtree

Happy With Fossils

H ave fun,
A t the beach,
P lease do,
P lease do,
Y es please do.

W hen you look around you think, *what can I do?*
I n the whole beach, there is nothing that suits you,
T hen you remember fossils!
H appily, you ask Dad, "Can I come with you?" and he
says yes.

F or every fossil you find your heart shines,
O h, we have to leave,
S ad to leave,
S o we'll come back again,
I t was very sad to leave,
L et's hope we go again,
S o we say goodbye.

Alastair North (7)
Plymtree CE Primary School, Plymtree

Dancing To Mars

D ance and prance all you like
A smear of magic may appear at night
N orthern Lights with sparkling stars
C lara and me, dancing to Mars
I am flying through the night
N ew unicorns glowing under the bright moonlight
G oing to sleep in Dream World.

Daisy Spicer (7)
Plymtree CE Primary School, Plymtree

Monsters

Monsters lurk in the dark,
Wings like an eagle,
And teeth like a shark.
Even though they look wild,
They're just friendly and mild,
Under the stairs,
And on spindly chairs,
Really they're scared of us.
So don't make a fuss,
Now remember, monsters are the best.

Dexter Spicer (8)
Plymtree CE Primary School, Plymtree

Mummy

M y mummy is the best mummy in the world.
U nder pressure, she doesn't do very good.
M y mummy is lots of fun.
M ummy is Mummy and I love her.
Y es I love Mummy.

Emily Blade (9)
Plymtree CE Primary School, Plymtree

My Wild And Curious Dreams

Once, in my dream, my thoughts were rushing through my head,
Whooshing around like waves on a breezy summer's day,
Throwing a beach ball with my friend,
Dancing like a sugar plum fairy underneath the sun's rays.

At about one in the morning, I saw a beautiful thing,
A diamond sparkling and gleaming, it had a lovely bling,
It made me want to shout and sing,
"Hallelujah! My lord, my king!"

At three, my vision was quite blurry, so I began to worry,
I wanted to scream, but nothing would come out,
My worries started to fly about,
I was getting out of control, my head was going to roll.

It was finally morning, I slept like a queen,
My dreams felt so powerful, but I couldn't remember them,
Was it December or September? That I'd never know,
Did I see a dog in a little pink bow?

Sophie White (10)
Regent House Prepartory School, Newtownards

Gratefulness

I dreamed a dream of a girl just like me
Who was fortunate enough to live out her dreams
She had forgotten to appreciate all that she had
And remember to think of people who need help or felt
sad
My family was not rich or poor
But we did know one thing for sure
Happiness came before all wealth
So we should think of those around us and do all we
can to help

As we set off on our holidays
I gave more thought to my carefree ways
I should take time to notice people around me here
Their happiness or sadness and fears
And this is how I would spend my days
Being a better me in Madagascar

We went to the market where I did see
A sad little girl cuddled up in a corner
I decided to approach her and said, "What's wrong?"
The little girl said nothing as she cried
The endless stream of tears flowing from her eyes

As I continued to stay quietly by her side
Eventually, she looked at me and said, "I'm lost."

I walked with her until we found her parents
The joy and grateful smiles on their faces
Made me realise that helping her helped me even more
And that feeling has made me even more sure
That I am grateful for all I have
And I love to help, I love to share
The everlasting joy of care.

Nina Miller (10)
Regent House Prepartory School, Newtownards

The Olympics

The Olympic rings on the wall in the distance,
The team stepped up to take the shot, silence,
A lot of frantic heads in hands,
While the manager pulled down on his pants,
"They've done it!" shouted the commentator,
Later on, the guns were shot,
Northern Ireland won by the shot.

Running, running round the track,
Once you start, you can't turn back,
"3, 2, 1," the officials shouted,
Quickly, the last watchers in the stadium crowded.

I presented to the judge,
The music played,
I did my routine,
And it went better than any practice I had before,
A final jump to try and land
Without a thump.

The sand was set,
Lines from the rake leaving faint lines,
Clapping with the onlookers, I prepare my mind,

Running towards the pit,
As fast as a cheetah,
Where will I land?

Rose Harper (11)
Regent House Prepartory School, Newtownards

Up In The Air

I walked out the door and felt something weird,
I looked at my feet, but wish I didn't peer,
My small feet started to lift,
The ground was getting further away,
My heart skipped a beat as I was right over the
motorway.

I wanted to scream, but I could not communicate,
I felt as light as a feather, but as heavy as a weight,
I started to wonder, was it my meal?
Was it a dream or something real?
I was so, so worried, I was biting my nails.

I was up in the air, no one seemed to care,
So I looked down, but didn't ever see a glare,
I hoped someone could save me, but that would be
useless,
I was too far up, I was everything but fearless,
I was sweating with fear, I started to fall,
As fast as lightning, I let out a call.

Hannah Poulter (11)
Regent House Prepartory School, Newtownards

He Shoots!

"Thomas Holroyd to get Leeds promoted!"
"If he doesn't score this, he'll be hated!"
"He's stepping up for the free-kick!
"The clock's ticking down, with all the Leeds fans on his back, can he do it?"

The Leeds fans watching with hope,
If he misses this, the team will go down a bad slope.
"He steps up to the stage, if he scores this, he's a mage,
Here we go!"
He shoots!
"Oh yes! he's done it! He strikes it beautifully on his right foot."

"He can be compared to the likes of Messi and R9!"
This must be an otherworldly sign,
I can't believe this, it's absolutely out of this world,
"He might be the best young player in the world."

Tom Holroyd (11)
Regent House Prepartory School, Newtownards

Somewhere Far Away!

I am driving in the car,
I am driving very far,
I have gotten to my destination,
It is a lovely location!
Now I'm out of the car,
I am in a rocket ship,
I'm zooming off to Mars,
I can see the stars and the pretty pink cars!
Then I go down to the floor,
I can almost see the door to my greatest vacation,
I have landed in Brazil,
But now I feel ill,
So I get back into my ship,
I fly another mile,
And now I am walking down my very own aisle,
Right into my cosy bed,
To read my favourite story,
It is called Buzz Buzz!
Oh, not the alarm clock!
It was all just a dream,
Why is reality so mean?

Darcy Gray (9)
Regent House Prepartory School, Newtownards

In The Forest

I went for a walk in the forest one day,
I looked around and saw the cutest baby wolf ever,
It was so cute.
I stroked the baby wolf,
It was so soft, it was as soft as a blanket.
I started to get hungry because I was walking for miles.
Then I saw the most beautiful display of chocolate
trees,
I took a big bite, I nearly jumped a mile because it was
so delicious,
But then what did I hear?
Oh, it was just Mum,
She said, "Wake up Marla, it's time to wake up."
Oh, how I would love to stay in that dreamy world.
But I can always go back tomorrow night!

Marla Gilmore (9)
Regent House Prepartory School, Newtownards

The Day We Found 04

Breaking news!
An astronaut has just discovered a new planet called
04
Now they are working towards a visit there
They also think aliens live there
Because there are doors with chores and apple cores
Now Buzz is on the rocket ship heading to 04
I wonder what he will see
When his feet touch the floor?
Aliens made of chocolate
Who love an ice cream treat
Oh, what a magical creature to meet
With eyes that glow like Wonka's special sweets
Living in trees taller than ten feet
Turns out we are not alone
In the Milky Way galaxy, we call our home!

Alexander Clements (9)
Regent House Prepartory School, Newtownards

The League Win

"The chance for Jude O'Hara!"
"Maybe as good as Kaká!"
Jude thought, *where do I put it?*
If I don't decide, I might have a fit.

With the penalty to win it,
He hits it with power and spins it,
To win the league for LFC,
Compared to the celebrating fans, he looks like a pet.

The Premier League lifted above his head,
This would be something he would remember to his deathbed,
By then, all of the City players had fled,
They were victors 'til the end.

Jude O'Hara (11)
Regent House Prepartory School, Newtownards

My Weird Dream

One day, I was in my bed,
I thought of a dream,
Now not in my bed and not in my room,
I was scared.
Who and where am I? How did I get here?
Is this even still the same year?
I was very far away,
Somewhere in my head,
Where there were loads of trees that were very, very
tall.

I was in a forest and in a beautiful place,
But I felt so lonely in the space.
So I went back to my bed,
I went back to sleep.
What a dream to be back home -
I was so happy,
I could weep!

Emilie Park (8)
Regent House Prepartory School, Newtownards

Nightmares

Late at night, I lie there in bed,
Thinking, thinking, thinking, thoughts flying round my
head,
Dreaming about one thing or another,
Then a monster ate my mother!
The night went on forever and ever,
My dreams are often very clever,
It was dark and scary all around,
Then I heard a curious sound...
I realised there was a storm,
A tornado was about to form,
Gazing at the tilted tree,
I prayed to God, "Please, help me!"
It then went blank and all was warm,
Soft and cosy in my dorm.

Ruby-Rose Roberts (10)
Regent House Prepartory School, Newtownards

I Just Flew!

There I lay,
In my garden,
And by the fence, sat my dog.
But when I looked again,
My dear sweet puppy
Was a polar bear!
I walked towards him
And put out my fist,
He sniffed it and lay down,
So I got on his back and slept.
I woke in the Arctic, on the great beast,
On a great cliff, at the very edge.
Suddenly, he jumped,
And I realised it felt like flying!
I felt ecstatic and free!
Suddenly, I awoke in bed,
Cosy and warm,
But I smiled,
As I just flew.

Christine Large (10)
Regent House Prepartory School, Newtownards

186

Untitled

Francesca and I are magical friends,
Fairies to be exact,
We flew out the window,
Oh how airy we were!
As our wings fluttered,
Me and my pal,
We lifted off and zoomed all the way to Portugal,
She shouted, "Oh how fun!"
With her mouth full of a chocolate bun,
Soon it was time to go,
We started to panic,
Back home our parents were getting frantic,
We flew back through the window,
Safe and sound,
I'll be glad to wake up with my feet on the ground!

Ella McDowell (9)
Regent House Prepartory School, Newtownards

The Land Of Dogs

The Land of Dogs is like a furry ball covered with
Labradors, cocker spaniels and poodles
I go there every night!
Until my dad comes and wakes me up
Poof! The dogs are gone!
Oh how I wish I could stay in the Land of Dogs
Maybe one day I'll wake up to find a furry puppy
sniffing me!
A spaniel? A poodle?
Oh, what could it be?
"Surprise!" my dad would say. Oh, what a day!
But no. The wonderful land is all just a dream.

Katie Turner (9)
Regent House Prepartory School, Newtownards

I Dreamed A Dream

One night, in my bed,
Many things in my head,
Stories of heroes, villains,
Monsters and astronauts.

I have superpowers to fly
Through the sky,
Shoot lasers,
And to eat waffles.

Now I'm floating in space,
A rocket close by,
A shooting star passes by,
I made a wish upon it too.

But now I'm in a dark place,
I'm very scared, but then...
I wake up,
Safely in my bed.

Bruce Rothwell (10)
Regent House Prepartory School, Newtownards

The Monster That Ate My Mother

It's big and hairy but not very scary.
It always makes me laugh.
A giggle and a roar when it opens the door.
Always... creeping... up behind me.
I
    fell
        down
on the ground.
I said, "I'm going to drown!"
My mother heard the drop.
She tried to make it stop.
And then the monster *ate* her!

William Rankin (9)
Regent House Prepartory School, Newtownards

Yummy World

As I step into the portal,
I suddenly feel a bit immortal.
When I'm being teleported,
I see something red.

Now I see, I am in my house,
With two pink pigs and one grey mouse.
Oh, and that thing looks red,
It turns out it is... chocolate bread.

Cillian Steensma (8)
Regent House Prepartory School, Newtownards

YoungWriters® Est. 1991

YOUNG WRITERS INFORMATION

We hope you have enjoyed reading this book – and that you will continue to in the coming years.

If you're a young writer who enjoys reading and creative writing, or the parent of an enthusiastic poet or story writer, do visit our website **www.youngwriters.co.uk**. Here you will find free competitions, workshops and games, as well as recommended reads, a poetry glossary and our blog.

If you would like to order further copies of this book, or any of our other titles, then please give us a call or visit **www.youngwriters.co.uk**.

Young Writers
Remus House
Coltsfoot Drive
Peterborough
PE2 9BF
(01733) 890066
info@youngwriters.co.uk

f YoungWritersUK **X** YoungWritersCW
◎ youngwriterscw **♪** youngwriterscw